German Short Stories for Beginners
Book 5

Over 100 Dialogues and Daily Used Phrases to Learn German in Your Car. Have Fun & Grow Your Vocabulary, with Crazy Effective Language Learning Lessons

www.LearnLikeNatives.com

© **Copyright 2020**

By Learn Like A Native

ALL RIGHTS RESERVED

No part of this book may be reproduced, stored in a retrieval system, or transmitted in any form or by any means, without the prior written permission of the publisher.

TABLE OF CONTENT

INTRODUCTION	5
CHAPTER 1 New Roommates	
/ Common everyday objects + possession	17
Translation of the Story	34
New Roommates	34
CHAPTER 2 A Day in the Life	
/ transition words	45
Translation of the Story	61
A Day in the Life	61
CHAPTER 3 The Camino Inspiration	
/ Numbers + Family	71
Translation of the Story	86
The Camino Inspiration	86
CONCLUSION	95
About the Author	101

INTRODUCTION

Before we dive into some German, I want to congratulate you, whether you're just beginning, continuing, or resuming your language learning journey. Here at Learn Like a Native, we understand the determination it takes to pick up a new language and after reading this book, you'll be another step closer to achieving your language goals.

As a thank you for learning with us, we are giving you free access to our 'Speak Like a Native' eBook. It's packed full of practical advice and insider tips on how to make language learning quick, easy, and most importantly, enjoyable. Head over to LearnLikeNatives.com to access your free guide and peruse our huge selection of language learning resources.

Learning a new language is a bit like cooking—you need several different ingredients and the right technique, but the end result is sure to be delicious. We created this book of short stories for learning German because language is alive. Language is about the senses—hearing, tasting the words on your tongue, and touching another culture up close. Learning a language in a classroom is a fine place to start, but it's not a complete introduction to a language.

In this book, you'll find a language come to life. These short stories are miniature immersions into the German language, at a level that is perfect for beginners. This book is not a lecture on grammar. It's not an endless vocabulary list. This book is the closest you can come to a language immersion without leaving the country. In the stories within, you will see people speaking to each other, going through daily life situations, and using the most common, helpful words and phrases in language.

You are holding the key to bringing your German studies to life.

Made for Beginners

We made this book with beginners in mind. You'll find that the language is simple, but not boring. Most of the book is in the present tense, so you will be able to focus on dialogues, root verbs, and understand and find patterns in subject-verb agreement.

This is not "just" a translated book. While reading novels and short stories translated into German is a wonderful thing, beginners (and even novices) often run into difficulty. Literary licenses and complex sentence structure can make reading in your second language truly difficult—not to mention BORING. That's why German Short Stories for Beginners is the perfect book to pick up. The stories are simple, but not infantile. They were not written for children, but the language is simple so that beginners can pick it up.

The Benefits of Learning a Second Language

If you have picked up this book, it's likely that you are already aware of the many benefits of learning a second language. Besides just being fun, knowing more than one language opens up a whole new world to you. You will be able to communicate with a much larger chunk of the world. Opportunities in the workforce will open up, and maybe even your day-to-day work will be improved. Improved communication can also help you expand your business. And from a neurological perspective, learning a second language is like taking your daily vitamins and eating well, for your brain!

How To Use The Book

The chapters of this book all follow the same structure:

- A short story with several dialogs
- A summary in German
- A list of important words and phrases and their English translation
- Questions to test your understanding
- Answers to check if you were right
- The English translation of the story to clear every doubt

You may use this book however is comfortable for you, but we have a few recommendations for getting the most out of the experience. Try these tips and if they work for you, you can use them on every chapter throughout the book.

1) Start by reading the story all the way through. Don't stop or get hung up on any particular words or phrases. See how much of the plot you can understand in this way. We think you'll get a lot more of it than you may expect, but it is completely normal not to understand everything in the story. You are learning a new language, and that takes time.

2) Read the summary in German. See if it matches what you have understood of the plot.

3) Read the story through again, slower this time. See if you can pick up the meaning of any words or phrases you don't understand by using context clues and the information from the summary.

4) Test yourself! Try to answer the five comprehension questions that come at the end of each story. Write your answers

down, and then check them against the answer key. How did you do? If you didn't get them all, no worries!

5) Look over the vocabulary list that accompanies the chapter. Are any of these the words you did not understand? Did you already know the meaning of some of them from your reading?

6) Now go through the story once more. Pay attention this time to the words and phrases you haven't understand. If you'd like, take the time to look them up to expand your meaning of the story. Every time you read over the story, you'll understand more and more.

7) Move on to the next chapter when you are ready.

Read and Listen

The audio version is the best way to experience this book, as you will hear a native German speaker tell you each story. You will become accustomed to their accent as you listen along, a huge plus for when you want to apply your new language skills in the real world.

If this has ignited your language learning passion and you are keen to find out what other resources are available, go to **LearnLikeNatives.com**, where you can access our vast range of free learning materials. Don't know where to begin? An excellent place to start is our 'Speak Like a Native' free eBook, full of practical advice and insider tips on how to make language learning quick, easy, and most importantly, enjoyable.

And remember, small steps add up to great advancements! No moment is better to begin learning than the present.

FREE BOOK!

Get the *FREE BOOK* that reveals the secrets path to learn any language fast, and without leaving your country.

Discover:

- The **language 5 golden rules** to master languages at will

- Proven **mind training techniques** to revolutionize your learning

- A complete step-by-step guide to **conquering any language**

CHAPTER 1
New Roommates /
Common everyday objects + possession

HANDLUNG

Heute ist Einzugstag an der Universität. Erstsemester bringen **ihre** Sachen in das Wohnheim.

Anna kommt mit ihren Eltern an der Universität an. **Ihr** Auto ist voller Kisten. Anna bringt alles mit, was sie für ein Schuljahr braucht. Sie parken außerhalb von Annas Wohnheim. Das Gebäude ist ein großes Backsteingebäude. Es sieht langweilig aus. Anna versucht positiv zu denken. Dieses Jahr wird toll, sagt sie sich.

Ihre Familie beginnt, das Auto zu entladen. Anna ist sehr gut vorbereitet. Sie nehmen Kartons mit ihren Sachen heraus. Ihr Bruder hilft ihr, die Kisten ins Zimmer zu bringen. Das Zimmer ist klein. Es gibt zwei Betten. Anna wird einen Mitbewohner haben.

Die erste Schachtel, die Anna öffnet, enthält Schulsachen. Sie legt ihre **Notizblöcke**, **Bleistifte** und **Kugelschreiber** auf ihren Schreibtisch. Der Raum hat keine Dekoration, außer einem **Fernseher** an der Wand. Anna organisiert ihre Sachen im Zimmer. Sie nimmt ihren **Kalender** heraus und hängt ihn an die Wand.

"Das ist nicht **mein** Kalender", sagt sie. Es ist ein Kalender voller schöner Frauen.

"Das ist **sein** Kalender", sagt Anna und zeigt auf ihren Bruder.

"Oh, tut mir leid", sagt ihr Bruder. Anna wirft ihn in den **Mülleimer**. Die Familie lacht.

Es klopft an der Tür. Sie öffnen die Tür. Ein blondes Mädchen steht draußen. Sie wird von einer älteren Frau begleitet, ihrer Mutter.

"Hallo, ich bin Beatriz", sagt das Mädchen.

"Ich bin Anna", sagt Anna. "Wir sind wohl Mitbewohner."

"Woher kommst du?" fragt Beatriz.

"Aus der Nähe, nur eine Stunde nördlich", sagt Anna.

"Ich auch!" sagt Beatriz.

Die Mädchen schütteln sich die Hand und lächeln. Beatriz bringt ihre eigenen Kisten. Die Familien helfen ihren Töchtern auszupacken.

Die ersten Tage der Schule sind schön. Anna findet neue Freunde. Sie und Beatriz verstehen sich gut. Anna geht in ihre neuen Kurse. Alles ist perfekt. Eine Sache ist jedoch komisch. Einige von Annas Sachen beginnen zu verschwinden. Erst kann sie ihre **Bürste** nicht finden. Dann, am nächsten Tag, schaut sie in den **Spiegel**. Sie sieht ihre **Lotion**, aber ihr **Parfüm** fehlt. Als sie am

Abend aus dem Unterricht kommt, legt sie Musik auf. Es gibt keinen Ton. Ihr **Lautsprecher** ist weg!

Sie fragt Beatriz. "Beatriz", sagt sie, "vermisst du etwas?"

"Ja!" sagt Beatriz. "Mein Laptop **Computer**. Ich drehe durch."

"Oh nein!" sagt Anna. "Mir fehlen auch ein paar Dinge."

Anna fehlen jetzt drei Sachen. Sie ruft ihre Mutter von ihrem **Handy** an.

"Hallo, Mama", sagt Anna.

"Hallo, Schatz", sagt ihre Mutter. "Wie ist die Schule?"

"Gut", sagt Anna. "Aber meine Sachen verschwinden."

"Was meinst du damit?" fragt ihre Mutter. Anna erzählt ihrer Mutter von dem fehlenden Parfüm, dem fehlenden Lautsprecher und der fehlenden Bürste.

"Das ist seltsam", sagt ihre Mutter: "Hast du sie irgendwohin mitgenommen?"

"Nein, Mama", sagt Anna. "Ich habe den Raum nie verlassen. Der Rest der **Stereoanlage** ist hier. Mein **MP3-Player** ist auch hier."

"Schließt du deine Tür ab?" fragt ihre Mutter.

"Ja, Mama!" sagt Anna. "Und es ist nur das Parfüm, das weg ist. Ich habe immer noch das ganze andere **Make-up**, **Lippenstift**, alles!"

"Könnte es Beatriz sein?" fragt ihre Mutter.

"Auf keinen Fall, sie vermisst auch Sachen", sagt Anna.

"Okay, geh zu den Fundsachen", sagt Annas Mutter.

"OK! Ich muss los", sagt Anna.

Anna legt auf. Die Idee ihrer Mutter ist gut. Sie geht nach unten ins Wohnheimbüro. Sie bittet darum, die Fundbox zu sehen. Die Box ist voll. Sie durchsucht sie. Sie findet **Notizbücher**, eine **Videokamera** und sogar einen **Kamm**. Aber sie findet ihre Sachen nicht. Sie sucht weiter. Sie sieht einen Laptop **Computer**.

"Ist das **ihrer**?" fragt sie sich und denkt an Beatriz. Sie zieht ihn heraus. Ist es! Sie nimmt den Computer, um ihn Beatriz zu geben. Wenigstens hat sie etwas gefunden.

Sie geht nach oben. Sie gibt Beatriz den Computer.

"Toll, Anna, das ist **mein** Computer!" sagt Beatriz. "Vielen Dank."

"Gern geschehen", sagt Anna. "Ich bin so froh, dass ich **deinen** Computer gefunden habe."

"Ich auch," sagt Beatriz. "Hast du irgendwas von deinen Sachen gefunden?"

"Nein", sagt Anna.

"Mist", sagt Beatriz. Die Mädchen gehen schlafen.

Am nächsten Tag hat Beatriz Unterricht. Anna bleibt im Wohnheimzimmer. Sie arbeitet an einem Projekt und benutzt eine **Schere**, um Bilder auf einen **Ordner** aufzukleben. Sie denkt über ihre fehlenden Gegenstände nach. Vielleicht sollte sie im Wohnheimzimmer nachsehen. Sie schaut überall nach. Dann dreht sie sich zu Beatrizs Schrank. Sie öffnet ihn. Sie schaut hinein.

"Das gehört mir!" sagt Anna. Sie zieht ihre Bürste raus. Sie ist schockiert. Warum ist ihre Bürste in Beatrizs Schrank? Sie schaut genauer hin. Unter einem Stapel von **Kleidern** fühlt sie etwas Hartes. Sie zieht es heraus. Es ist ihre Flasche Parfüm! Als sie noch genauer hinschaut, findet sie auch ihren Lautsprecher.

"Es war die ganze Zeit Beatriz", sagt Anna. Das Zimmer**telefon** klingelt. Anna antwortet. Es ist Beatrizs Mutter.

"Hallo, Anna", sagt Beatrizs Mutter. "Wie geht's dir?"

"Gut", sagt Anna. "Beatriz ist nicht hier."

"Kannst du ihr sagen, dass ich angerufen habe?" fragt Beatrizs Mutter.

"Ja, aber kann ich mit Ihnen über etwas reden?" fragt Anna.

"Sicher", sagt Beatrizs Mutter.

"Einige meiner Sachen sind verschwunden", sagt Anna, "und ich habe gerade einige davon im Schrank **Ihrer** Tochter gefunden."

"Oh, nein", sagt Beatrizs Mutter. "Ich muss dir etwas sagen."

"Was?" sagt Anna.

"Beatriz ist eine Kleptomanin", sagt ihre Mutter. "Sie nimmt Dinge und bringt sie dann genau sieben Tage später zurück. Sie wird dir die Sachen bis morgen zurückgeben."

"Was soll ich tun?" fragt Anna.

"Warte, bis sie sie zurückbringt", sagt ihre Mutter.

"Okay", sagt Anna.

"Danke für dein Verständnis", sagt Beatrizs Mutter.

ZUSAMMENFASSUNG

Anna und Beatriz sind Mitbewohnerinnen. Es ist ihr erstes Jahr an der Universität. Sie begegnen sich am Einzugstag. Sie richten sich ihr Wohnheimzimmer ein. Ihre Eltern helfen. Sie verstehen sich gut. Während der ersten Woche verschwinden viele von Annas Sachen. Sie kann sie nirgends finden. Beatriz hat auch einige fehlenden Sachen. Anna sucht überall. Sie sucht in den Fundsachen, wo sie Beatrizs vermissten Computer findet. Als Beatriz nicht da ist, schaut Anna in ihren Schrank. Sie findet alle ihre Sachen.

Beatrizs Mutter ruft an. Sie erzählt Anna, dass Beatriz eine Kleptomanin ist.

VOKABELLISTE

ihre	their
ihr	her
Kisten	boxes
mein	mine
Notizblöcke	notepads
Bleistifte	pencils
Kugelschreiber	pens
Fernseher	television
Kalender	calendar
sein	his
Mülleimer	trash can
Bürste	brush

Spiegel	mirror
Lotion	lotion
Parfüm	perfume
Lautsprecher	speaker
Computer	computer
Handy	cell phone
Stereoanlage	stereo system
Make-up	makeup
Lippenstift	lipstick
Notizbuch	notebook
Videokamera	video camera
Kamm	comb
mein	my
ihrer	yours
deinen	your
Schere	scissors

Kleider	clothes
Telefon	telephone
ihrer	your

FRAGEN

1) Woher kennen sich Beatriz und Anna?

    a) sie sind schon immer befreundet

    b) sie treffen sich im Unterricht

    c) sie sind Mitbewohner

    d) sie gehen auf die selbe Schule

2) Welcher dieser Gegenstände ist nicht verschwunden?

    a) Bürste

    b) Parfüm

    c) Lautsprecher

d) Spiegel

3) Was schlägt Annas Mutter vor?

    a) dass Anna nach Hause kommt

    b) dass Anna Beatriz konfrontiert

    c) dass Anna eine neue Bürste kauft

    d) dass Anna im Fundbüro nachschaut

4) Was findet Anna im Fundbüro?

    a) ihre Bürste

    b) Beatrizs Computer

    c) ein Sweatshirt

    d) ihr Parfüm

5) Was ist mit Annas Sachen passiert?

    a) Beatriz nahm sie und legte sie in ihren Schrank

b) Anna verlor sie

c) Anna hat sie weggeworfen

d) nichts

ANSWERS

1) Woher kennen sich Beatriz und Anna?

    c) sie sind Mitbewohner

2) Welcher dieser Gegenstände ist nicht verschwunden?

    d) Spiegel

3) Was schlägt Annas Mutter vor?

    d) dass Anna im Fundbüro nachschaut

4) Was findet Anna im Fundbüro?

    b) Beatrizs Computer

5) Was ist mit Annas Sachen passiert?

    a) Beatriz nahm sie und legte sie in ihren Schrank

Translation of the Story

New Roommates

STORY

Today is move-in day at the university. First year students move **their** things into the dormitory.

Anna arrives to the university with her parents. **Her** car is loaded with **boxes**. Anna brings everything she needs for a year of school with her. They park outside of Anna's dormitory. The building is a big, brick building. It looks boring. Anna tries to think positive. This year will be great, she tells herself.

Her family begins to unload the car. Anna is very prepared. They take out boxes full of her things. Her brother helps her take the boxes up to the room. The room is small. There are two beds. Anna will have a roommate.

The first box Anna opens has school supplies. She puts her **notepads**, **pencils** and **pens** on her desk. The room has no decoration, except for a **television** on the wall. Anna organizes her things in the room. She takes her **calendar** out to put on the wall.

"This isn't **mine**!" she says. It is a calendar of pretty women.

"This is **his**," Anna says, pointing at her brother.

"Oh, sorry," says her brother. Anna throws it in the **trash can**. The family laughs.

There is a knock on the door. They open the door. A blonde girl stands outside. She is with an older woman, her mother.

"Hello, I'm Beatriz," says the girl.

"I'm Anna," says Anna. "I guess we are roommates!"

"Where are you from?" asks Beatriz.

"Nearby, just an hour north," says Anna.

"Me too!" says Beatriz.

The girls shake hands and smile. Beatriz brings her own boxes. The families help their daughters unpack.

The first days of school are nice. Anna makes new friends. She and Beatriz get along great. Anna goes to her new classes. Everything is perfect. However, one thing is wrong. Some of Anna's belongings begin to disappear. First, she can't find her **brush**. Then, the next day, she looks in the **mirror**. She sees her **lotion** but her **perfume** is missing. When she arrives from class that evening, she puts on some music. There is no sound. Her **speaker** is gone!

She asks Beatriz. "Beatriz," she says. "Are you missing anything?"

"Yes!" says Beatriz. "My laptop **computer**. I am freaking out."

"Oh no!" says Anna. "I am missing a few things, too."

Anna is missing three things now. She calls her mother on her **cell phone**.

"Hi, mom," says Anna.

"Hi, honey," says her mom. "How is school?"

"Fine," says Anna. "But my belongings keep disappearing."

"What do you mean?" asks her mom. Anna tells her mom about the missing perfume, the missing speaker, and the missing brush.

"That is so strange," says her mom. "Did you take them somewhere?"

"No, mom," says Anna. "I never left the room. The rest of the **stereo system** is here. My **mp3 player,** too."

"Do you lock your door?" asks her mom.

"Yes, mom!" says Anna. "And it's just the perfume that is gone. I still have all the other **makeup**, **lipstick**, everything!"

"Do you think it could be Beatriz?" asks her mom.

"No way, she is missing stuff too," says Anna.

"Ok, go check the lost-and-found," says Anna's mom.

"Ok! Gotta go," says Anna.

Anna hangs up the phone. Her mom's idea is good. She goes downstairs to the dormitory office. She asks to see the lost-and-found box. The box is full. She looks through it. She finds **notebooks**, a **video camera**, and even a **comb**. But does not see her things. She looks more. She sees a laptop **computer**.

"Is that **yours**?" she asks, thinking of Beatriz. She pulls it out. It is. She takes the computer to give to Beatriz. At least she finds something.

She goes upstairs. She gives Beatriz the computer.

"Wow, Anna, it's **my** computer!" says Beatriz. "Thank you so much."

"You're welcome," says Anna. "So glad I found **your** computer."

"Me too," says Beatriz. "Did you find any of your things?"

"No," says Anna.

"Bummer," says Beatriz. The girls go to sleep.

The next day, Beatriz has class. Anna stays in the dorm room. She works on a project, using **scissors** to cut pictures to glue on a **folder**. She thinks about her missing items. Maybe she should look in the dorm room. She looks everywhere. Then she turns to Beatriz's closet. She opens it. She looks inside it.

"This is mine!" says Anna. She pulls out her brush. She is shocked. Why is her brush in Beatriz's closet? She looks closer. Under a stack of **clothes**, she feels something hard. She pulls it out. It is her bottle of perfume! When she looks closer, she finds her speaker, too.

"It was Beatriz the whole time," says Anna. The room **telephone** rings. Anna answers. It is Beatriz's mom.

"Hi, Anna," says Beatriz's mom. "How are you?"

"Fine," says Anna. "Beatriz isn't here."

"Can you tell her I called?" asks Beatriz's mom.

"Yes, but, can I talk to you about something?" asks Anna.

"Sure," says Beatriz's mom.

"Some of my things have gone missing," says Anna. "And I just found many of them in **your** daughter's closet."

"Oh, no," says Beatriz's mom. "I need to tell you something."

"What?" says Anna.

"Beatriz is a kleptomaniac," says her mom. "She takes things and then returns them exactly seven days later. She will return those items to you by tomorrow."

"What do I do?" asks Anna.

"Just wait for her to return them," says her mom.

"Okay," says Anna.

"Thank you for understanding," says Beatriz's mom.

CHAPTER 2
A Day in the Life / transition words

HANDLUNG

Bey wacht in einem Hotelzimmer auf. Sie ist müde. Ihr Körper ist müde, **aber** ihr Geist ist noch müder. Sie fühlt sich allein. Ihre Freunde und Familie verstehen nicht, wie es ist, berühmt zu sein. Sie lacht. Sie wollen berühmt sein. Sie wollen einen Tag in ihrem Leben verbringen. Die Leute denken, dass Prominente den ganzen Tag Spaß haben. Sie denken, dass Prominente alles bekommen, was sie wollen. Bey weiß **jedoch**, dass das nicht stimmt.

Warum wollen Menschen berühmt sein? Denkt Bey. Sie macht einen Kaffee. Die Medien zeigen ihren Erfolg. Menschen wollen Erfolgreich sein. Sie wollen ein perfektes Leben. **Infolgedessen** versuchen sie berühmt zu werden. Sie weiß, dass das Leben nicht perfekt ist.

Die Uhr zeigt sieben Uhr. Ihr Tag ist hektisch. **Deshalb** muss sie früh aufstehen. Manche Leute denken, dass Prominente lange schlafen. Sie hat viel zu tun. Es ist keine Zeit, auszuschlafen. Sie hört die Türklingel.

"Hallo", sagt Bey.

"Hallo, Bey," sagen die drei Frauen. Sie gehen rein. Eine Frau ist ihre Stylistin. Eine andere Frau ist ihre Visagistin. **Zuletzt** tritt die Friseurin ein. Sie beginnen zu arbeiten.

"Welches Hemd?", sagt die Stylistin.

"Welche Lippenstiftfarbe?" fragt die Visagistin.

"Warum hast du so mit deinen Haaren geschlafen?", fragt die Friseurin.

Beys Kaffee ist kalt. Sie macht noch einen Kaffee. **Dann** beantwortet sie alle Fragen. Sie helfen ihr. **Endlich** ist sie fertig.

Sie verlässt das Hotel um 10 Uhr. Draußen sind viele Leute. Sie warten auf sie. Als sie rausgeht, schreien sie. Sie machen Fotos. Bey steigt in ein Auto. Das Auto hat dunkle Fenster. Niemand kann hineinsehen. **Darum** kann sie drinne tun, was sie will. Sie entspannt sich. Ihr Telefon klingelt.

"Hallo?" sagt sie.

"Bey, wo bist du?" fragt ihr Manager.

"Im Auto", sagt sie.

"Du bist zu spät!" sagt der Manager.

"Tut mir leid", sagt Bey. Sie hat Tanzunterricht, Gesangsunterricht und ein Fotoshooting. Ein anstrengender Tag. Ihr Manager kümmert sich um ihren Tagesablauf. Er sagt ihr, was sie zu tun hat. Er sagt ihr, wohin sie gehen soll. Sie fühlt sich gefangen. Sie muss arbeiten, um berühmt zu bleiben. Sie kann keinen Urlaub nehmen.

Das Auto hält an. **Als erstes** hat Bey ein Fotoshooting. Es ist für eine Zeitschrift. Ein Mädchen schminkt Bey. Sie ist ein Fan. Sie lächelt.

"Wie geht es Ihnen?" fragt sie.

"Gut", sagt Bey.

"Ich bin Ihr Fan", sagt sie.

"Danke", sagt Bey.

"Ich singe auch", sagt das Mädchen. Sie pudert Bey das Gesicht.

"Wirklich?" sagt Bey. Sie langweilt sich.

"Ja, ich will berühmt werden!" sagt das Mädchen.

"Berühmt zu sein ist viel Arbeit!" sagt Bey.

"Ist mir egal!" sagt das Mädchen.

"Was machst du heute Abend?" fragt Bey.

"Abendessen mit meinem Freund, einen Spaziergang im Park, vielleicht ein Museum besuchen", sagt das Mädchen.

"Ich habe Arbeit, ein Konzert", sagt Bey. "**Eigentlich** habe ich jeden Abend eins. Ich kann nicht in den Park gehen, **weil** die Leute mich erkennen. Sie lassen mich nicht in Ruhe."

"Oh", sagt das Mädchen. Sie macht das Make-up fertig.

"**Zum Beispiel** kann ich mich nicht erinnern wann ich das letzt Mal ein Museum besucht habe", sagt Bey. Sie ist fertig. Sie fotografiert sie. Ihr

Kleid ist bezaubernd. Sie sieht wunderschön und glücklich aus. Sie verabschiedet sich und steigt ins Auto.

Als **zweites** hat Bey Tanzunterricht. Sie übt in einem Tanzstudio. Ihre Lehrerin ist ein Profi. Sie üben für das Konzert. Das heutige Konzert ist in einem Stadion in New York City. Sie vergisst die Tanzschritte für ihren berühmtesten Song. Sie übt zwei Stunden lang. **Zweifellos** beherrscht sie den Tanz jetzt.

Als **drittes** hat Bey Stimmunterricht. Berühmte Sänger brauchen Unterricht. Stimmunterricht hilft ihnen, leichter zu singen. Das ist wichtig. **Immerhin** ist es schwierig, jeden Abend ein Konzert zu geben.

Nach dem Stimmunterricht isst sie zu Mittag. Ihre Assistentin bringt es ihr. Auch wenn es schnell geht, ist es gesund. Sie hat einen Smoothie und einen Salat. Bald muss sie sich auf das Konzert vorbereiten.

Sie überprüft ihr Mobiltelefon. Bey hat einen weiteren Assistenten. Dieser Assistent kümmert sich um soziale Medien. Sie stellt Bilder auf Instagram und Facebook. **Letztendlich** möchte sich Bey gerne selbst überzeugen. Ihr neues Bild hat 1.000.000 likes. Nicht schlecht, denkt sie. Es hat auch viele Kommentare. Manche sind gemein, **deshalb** schaltet Bey ihr Handy aus. sie versucht, positiv zu bleiben.

Im Auto ruft Bey ihre Freunde an. Sie spricht mit ihrer Mutter. Sie telefoniert im Auto, **da** sie nicht viel Zeit hat. Sie ist müde. Sie hat Kopfschmerzen. Vielleicht kann sie ein Nickerchen machen. Sie schaut auf ihr Handy. Es ist zu spät, um ein Nickerchen zu machen.

Während Bey sich bereit macht, warten die Fans. Draußen bildet sich eine Schlange. Sie sind aufgeregt. Sie haben eine Menge Geld für die Tickets bezahlt.

Jetzt schmerzt ihr Hals. Sie trinkt warmen Tee. **Wenn** sie nicht singen kann, werden die Fans traurig sein. Sie schaut auf ihr Telefon. Sie hat ein Bild für diese Momente gespeichert. Es ist ein Brief.

"Liebe Bey", steht da.

"Du bist meine Lieblingssängerin. Ich denke, du bist erstaunlich. Ich möchte wie du sein, wenn ich groß bin. In Liebe, Susy." Es ist von einem 7-jährigen Fan. Bey erinnert sich an sie. Sie lächelt. Es gibt Hunderte von Mädchen wie Susy beim Konzert. **Aus diesem Grund** tritt sie auf.

Schlussendlich endet das Konzert.

Immer mehr Fans bitten um ein Autogramm von Bey. Sie lächeln. Sie machen Fotos mit ihren Handys. Sie stellt sich ihre Leben vor. Sie gehen auf Partys. Sie treffen Freunde. Sie gehen in Restaurants. **Jedenfalls** haben sie die Wahl. Sie ist eifersüchtig. **Obwohl** sie nicht berühmt sind, haben sie ein besseres Leben.

Sie denkt an das Make-up-Mädchen von heute. Sie fragt sich, was sie jetzt macht? Bey denkt darüber nach auszusteigen.

Ganz plötzlich macht ihr Telefon ein Geräusch.

Es ist eine Erinnerung daran, ins Bett zu gehen. Morgen ist wieder ein stressiger Tag.

ZUSAMMENFASSUNG

Bey ist Prominent. Sie ist eine berühmte Popsängerin. Die Leute sind eifersüchtig auf ihr Leben. Es ist jedoch nicht einfach. Ihr Tag beginnt früh. Ihre drei Assistenten kommen ins Hotel. Sie machen sie fertig. Dann hat sie einen anstrengenden Tag. Sie hat ein Fotoshooting. Das Make-up-Mädchen will berühmt sein. Bey erklärt, dass es ist nicht so großartig ist. Bey nimmt Tanz- und Gesangsunterricht. Dann macht sie sich bereit für ihr Konzert. Sie fühlt sich krank. Sie tritt jedoch für ihre vielen Fans auf. Sie posiert für Fotos und gibt Autogramme. Sie ist eifersüchtig auf das normale Leben ihrer Fans.

VOKABELLISTE

aber	but
jedoch	however
infolgedessen	as a result

deshalb	therefore
zuletzt	lastly
dann	then
endlich	finally
darum	therefore
erstes	first
eigentlich	in fact
weil	because
zum Beispiel	for example
zweites	second
zweifellos	without a doubt
immerhin	after all
obwohl	even though
letztendlich	ultimately
deshalb	so
da	since

whärend	while
wenn	if
aus diesem Grund	for this reason
schlussendlich	eventually
jedenfalls	either way
obwohl	despite
ganz plötzlich	all of a sudden
drittes	third

FRAGEN

1) Welche Person kommt nicht zu Beys Hotel?

    a) eine Visagistin

    b) ein Stylist

    c) ein Fan

    d) ein Friseur

2) Warum ruft Beys Manager sie an?

    a) zu fragen, wo sie ist

    b) sie zu entlassen

    c) ihr zu gratulieren

    d) zu fragen, wie es ihr geht

3) Was ist Beys Job?

    a) Tänzerin

    b) Popstar

    c) Talk-Show-Host

    d) Fotografin

4) Was hilft Bey beim Singen?

    a) Tee trinken

    b) zum Sprachunterricht gehen

    c) beten

d) Finger kreuzen

5) Was bedeutet das Geräusch vom Telefon am Ende der Geschichte?

    a) jemand ruft an

    b) es ist an der Zeit für ihre Medikamente

    c) eine Benachrichtigung von Instagram

    d) es ist Zeit, ins Bett zu gehen

ANTWORTEN

1) Welche Person kommt nicht zu Beys Hotel?

    c) ein Fan

2) Warum ruft Beys Manager sie an?

a) zu fragen, wo sie ist

3) Was ist Beys Job?

b) Popstar

4) Was hilft Bey beim Singen?

b) sie geht zum Sprachunterricht

5) Was bedeutet das Geräusch vom Telefon am Ende der Geschichte?

d) es ist Zeit, ins Bett zu gehen

Translation of the Story

A Day in the Life

STORY

Bey wakes up in a hotel room. She is tired. Her body is tired, **but** her mind is more tired. She feels alone. Her friends and family don't understand what it is like to be famous. She laughs. They want to be famous. They want to spend a day in her life. People think celebrities have fun all day. They think celebrities get anything they want. **However,** Bey knows this is not true.

Why do people want to be famous? Bey thinks. She makes a coffee. The media shows her as success. People want success. They want a perfect life. **As a result,** they try to become famous. She knows life is not perfect.

The clock says seven o'clock. Her day is busy. **Therefore**, she has to wake up early. Some people think celebrities sleep late. She has a lot to do. There is no time to sleep late. She hears the doorbell.

"Hello," says Bey.

"Hi, Bey," say the three women. One woman is her stylist. Another woman is her makeup artist. **Lastly**, the hairdresser enters. She opens the door. They go inside. They begin to work.

"Which shirt?" says the stylist.

"Which color of lipstick?" asks the makeup artist.

"Why did you sleep with your hair like that?" asks the hairdresser.

Bey's coffee is cold. She makes another coffee. **Then**, she answers all the questions. They help her. **Finally,** she is ready.

She leaves the hotel at 10 a.m. There are many people outside. They wait for her. When she goes out, they scream. They take pictures. Bey gets in a car. The car has dark windows. No one can see in. **Therefore,** she can do what she wants. She relaxes. Her phone rings.

"Hello?" she says.

"Bey, where are you?" asks her manager.

"In the car," she says.

"You're late!" says the manager.

"Sorry," said Bey. She has dance practice, voice lessons, and a photo shoot. A busy day. Her manager keeps her schedule. He tells her what to do. He tells her when to go. She feels stuck. She must work to stay famous. She can't take a vacation.

The car stops. **First**, Bey has a photo shoot. It is for a magazine. A girl puts makeup on Bey. She is a fan. She smiles.

"How are you?" she asks.

"Fine," says Bey.

"I am your fan," she says.

"Thank you," says Bey.

"I sing, too," the girl says. She powders Bey's face.

"Really?" asks Bey. She is bored.

"Yes. I want to be famous!" says the girl.

"Being famous is a lot of work!" says Bey.

"I don't care!" says the girl.

"What are you doing tonight?" asks Bey.

"Dinner with my boyfriend, a walk in the park, maybe visit a museum," says the girl.

"I have work, a concert," says Bey. "**In fact,** I have one every night. I can't go out to the park **because** people recognize me. They don't leave me alone."

"Oh," says the girl. She finishes the makeup.

"**For example**, I can't remember a visit to a museum," says Bey. She is finished. She takes her pictures. Her dress is glamorous. She looks beautiful and happy. She says goodbye and gets in the car.

Second, Bey has dance practice. She practices in a dance studio. Her teacher is professional. They practice for the concert. Tonight's concert is in a stadium in New York City. She forgets the dance for her most famous song. She practices for two hours. **Without a doubt**, she knows the dance.

Third, Bey has voice lessons. Famous singers need lessons. Voice lessons help them sing easily. This is important. **After all,** singing a concert every night is difficult.

After voice, she eats lunch. Her assistant brings it to her. Even though it is quick, it is healthy. She has a smoothie and a salad. Soon she must prepare for the concert.

She checks her phone. Bey has another assistant. This assistant does social media. She puts pictures on Instagram and Facebook. **Ultimately**, Bey likes to see for herself. Her new picture has 1,000,000 likes. Not bad, she thinks. It also has many comments. Some are mean, **so** Bey turns off her phone. She tries to be positive.

In the car, Bey calls her friends. She talks to her mother. She talks in the car **since** she doesn't have much time. She is tired. She has a headache. Maybe she can nap. She looks at her phone. It is too late to nap.

While Bey gets ready, fans wait. They make a line outside. They are excited. They paid a lot of money for the tickets.

Now her throat hurts. She drinks warm tea. **If** she can't sing, the fans will be sad. She looks at her phone. She has a picture saved for these moments. It is a letter.

"Dear Bey," it says.

"You are my favorite singer. I think you are amazing. I want to be just like you when I grow up. Love, Susy." It is from a 7-year-old fan. Bey remembers her. She smiles. There are hundreds of girls like Susy at the concert. **For this reason,** she performs.

Eventually, the concert ends.

More and more fans ask for Bey's autograph. They smile. They take pictures on their phone. She imagines their lives. They go to parties. They see friends. They go to restaurants. **Either way**, they have freedom. She is jealous. **Despite** not being famous, they have better lives.

She thinks of the makeup girl from today. She wonders, what is she doing now? Bey thinks maybe she will quit.

All of a sudden, her phone makes a sound.

It is a reminder to go to bed. Tomorrow is another busy day.

CHAPTER 3
The Camino Inspiration / Numbers + Family

HANDLUNG

Molly liebt Abenteuer.

Sie ist das tapferste Mitglied ihrer **Familie**, sogar mutiger als ihre **beiden Brüder**. Sie geht oft mit ihrer Familie im Wald zelten. Dieses Wochenende gehen sie zusammen in die Berge. Der Mond scheint und die Vögel und Tiere sind ruhig. Molly sitzt mit ihren Brüdern und ihrer **Schwester** am Lagerfeuer. Sie reden und musizieren. Sie sehen eine Fledermaus über ihre Köpfe fliegen.

"Ihhh!" ruft Mollys Schwester.

"Eine Fledermaus!" ruft **einer** von Mollys Brüdern.

Plötzlich fliegen **drei** weitere Fledermäuse über ihre Köpfe.

"Ahhh! Lasst uns **Mama** und **Papa** holen!" ruft der andere Bruder, John.

"Es ist nur eine Fledermaus", sagt Molly.

Es kommen noch mehr Fledermäuse an, bis **acht** über ihnen fliegen. Mollys Schwester und Brüder verschwinden in ihren Zelten, zu Tode erschreckt. Molly bewegt sich nicht. Sie sieht zu, wie die Fledermäuse kreisen, jetzt **neunzehn**, nein, **zwanzig**!

"Hallo, Molly", sagt ihre **Mutter**, als sie hinter ihrem **Vater** zum Lagerfeuer geht.

"Beeindruckend, es gibt wirklich viele Fledermäuse in diesen Wäldern", sagt ihr Vater. "Hast du keine Angst?"

Molly schüttelte den Kopf und sieht zu, wie die Fledermäuse in den sternenklaren Nachthimmel fliegen.

"Lasst uns essen!" sagte sie. Ihre Brüder und Schwester kommen aus ihren Zelten. Die Familie isst am Feuer. Sie lieben es, zusammen zu zelten.

Molly ist **zweiundzwanzig**. Sie hat gerade ihr Studium abgeschlossen, wo sie Ingenieurwesen studierte. Sie hat keinen Job in einem Büro gefunden, also arbeitet sie in ihrem örtlichen

Outdoor-Laden. Sie spart sich ihr Gehalt und redet den ganzen Tag über ihr Lieblingshobby: Camping.

Jeden Samstag arbeitet Molly im **zweiten** Stock, mit allen Zelten, Rucksäcken und Campingutensilien. Diesen Samstag betritt ihr **Cousin** den Laden.

"Hallo, Jim!" sagt Molly, ein glückliches Lächeln auf ihrem Gesicht.

"Molly! Ich vergaß, dass du hier arbeitest", sagt Jim, der **dreißig** Jahre alte **Sohn** von Mollys **Tante** Jane.

"Wie geht es Tante Jane und **Onkel** Joe?" fragt Molly.

"Es geht ihnen gut. Dieses Wochenende besuchen sie **Großmutter** Gloria", sagt Jim. "Ich bin hier, um ein paar Sachen für eine Reise zu kaufen."

"Oh, sicher! Ich kann dir helfen. Was ist auf deiner Liste?" fragt Molly.

Jim zeigt Molly ein Stück Papier mit einer Liste von **fünfzehn** Gegenständen. Ein leichter Rucksack, ein Campingkocher, **vier** Paar warme Socken, Wanderstöcke, Allzweckseife, ein Taschenmesser und **achtzehn** Trockenmahlzeiten für unterwegs.

Beeindruckend, das klingt nach einer ziemlichen Reise, denkt Molly.

"Gib mir den leichtesten Rucksack, den du hast", sagt Jim. "Das Leichteste von allem, eigentlich.

Ich muss das Gewicht meines Rucksacks unter **achtundzwanzig** Pfund halten."

"Wofür kaufst du das alles?" fragt Molly, als sie mit Jim zu einer Wand geht, die mit Rucksäcken aller Farben bestückt ist, groß und klein.

"Ich gehe wandern", sagt Jim. "Quer durch Spanien."

Jim probiert die verschiedenen Rucksäcke aus. Er wählt Mollys Favoriten, einen roten Rucksack mit **sieben** Taschen, vier auf der Rückseite und drei innen. Der Rucksack ist so leicht, dass er kaum **zweieinhalb** Pfund wiegt. Er trägt ihn auf seinen Schultern, während er Molly in die Kleiderabteilung folgt.

"Es heißt Jakobsweg", erzählt Jim Molly. Ihr Cousin erzählt ihr von der Wanderung. Es ist eine Pilgerreise zur Kathedrale von Santiago de Compostela in Galicien. Man sagt, dass der Heilige Jakobus in der Kirche begraben ist.

Ihr Cousin Jim wird die Wanderung vom üblichen Ausgangspunkt des Französischen Wegs, Saint-Jean-Pied-de-Port, aus gehen. Von dort sind es etwa **fünfhundert** Kilometer nach Santiago. Die Wallfahrt ist seit dem Mittelalter beliebt. Kriminelle und andere Menschen gingen den Weg im Austausch für den Segen Gottes. Heutzutage reisen die meisten zu Fuß. Manche Menschen reisen mit dem Fahrrad. Ein paar Pilger reisen sogar auf einem Pferd oder Esel. Die Pilgerreise war religiös, aber heute machen es viele zur sportlichen Aktivität oder aus Reiselust.

"Ich muss reisen", sagt Jim. "Ich brauche Zeit zum Nachdenken. 500 Meilen zu gehen kann sehr spirituell sein."

Molly hilft Jim bei der Suche nach einer wasserdichten Jacke und einer Hose, die sich zu einer kurzen Hose öffnen lässt. Er scheint sehr glücklich mit seiner großen Tasche von Dingen. Er hat viel mehr in der Hand als die anderen Käufer. Er geht auf eine richtige Reise.

"Das macht **dreihundertsiebenundvierzig** Dollar und **sechsundsechzig** Cent", sagt Molly.

"Danke, Molly", sagt Jim.

Molly beginnt nachzudenken. Sie lebt zu Hause bei ihren **Eltern**. Ihre Mutter arbeitet als Richterin im örtlichen Gerichtsgebäude und ihr

Vater ist Anwalt. Sie sind beide selten zum Abendessen zu Hause. Sie bleiben bis spät abends im Büro. Ihre **Geschwister** leben mit ihren Familien in Seattle, drei Stunden entfernt. Sie ist allein, ohne richtigen Job. Sie hat niemanden, der sie aufhält.

Es wird der perfekte Urlaub. Und vielleicht entscheidet sie, was sie mit dem Rest ihres Lebens macht.

Warum nicht?

An diesem Tag beschließt Mollly, dass sie auf dem Jakobsweg wandern wird. Ab September, in drei Monaten. Allein.

ZUSAMMENFASSUNG

Eine junge Frau namens Molly liebt die Natur. Sie und ihre Familie campen oft zusammen. Sie arbeitet in einem Outdoor-Laden, während sie einen Job sucht der ihren Studium entspricht. Ihr Cousin Jim versucht eine Reise vorzubereiten. Er wird den Jakobsweg bestreiten und braucht Ausrüstung. Molly hilft ihm, einen Rucksack, Schuhe und alles andere zu kaufen, was er braucht. Sie beschließt, selbst den Jakobsweg zu gehen.

VOKABELLISTE

Familie	family
zwei	two
Bruder	brother
Schwester	sister
eins	one
drei	three

Mama	mom
Papa	dad
acht	eight
neunzehn	nineteen
zwanzig	twenty
Mutter	mother
Vater	father
zweiundzwanzig	twenty-two
zweiter	second
Cousin	cousin
dreißig	thirty
Sohn	son
Tante	aunt
Onkel	uncle
Großmutter	grandma
fünfzehn	fifteen

vier	four
achtzehn	eighteen
achtundzwanzig	twenty-eight
sieben	seven
zweieinhalb	two-and-a-half
fünfhundert	five hundred
dreihundert	three hundred
siebenundvierzig	forty-seven
sechsundsechzig	sixty-six
Eltern	parents
Geschwister	siblings

FRAGEN

1) Was hat Molly an der Universität studiert?

a) Kosmetik

b) Literatur

c) Ingenieurwesen

d) Marketing

2) Wie viele Geschwister hat Molly?

a) ein

b) zwei

c) drei

d) vier

3) Wie ist Jim mit Molly verwandt?

a) Bruder

b) Cousin

c) Großvater

d) Papa

4) Was ist der Jakobsweg?

    a) ein Pilgerweg

    b) eine Stadt

    c) einer Kirche

    d) ein Urlaub

5) Woher kommt Molly?

    a) die Vereinigten Staaten

    b) England

    c) Australia

    d) Frankreich

ANTWORTEN

1) Was hat Molly an der Universität studiert?

    c) Ingenieurwesen

2) Wie viele Geschwister hat Molly?

    c) drei

3) Wie ist Jim mit Molly verwandt?

    b) Cousin

4) Was ist der Jakobsweg?

    a) ein Pilgerweg

5) Woher kommt Molly?

    a) die Vereinigten Staaten

Translation of the Story

The Camino Inspiration

Molly loves adventures.

She is the bravest member of her **family**, even braver than her **two brothers**. She often goes camping with her family in the woods. This weekend, they go to the mountain together. The moon shines and the birds and animals are quiet. Molly sits with her brothers and her **sister** by the fire, talking and playing. They see a bat fly over their heads.

"Ewww!" shouts Molly's sister.

"A bat!" yells **one** of Molly's brothers.

Then, **three** more bats fly over their heads.

"Ahhh! Let's get **mom** and **dad**!" shouts the other brother, John.

"It's only a bat," says Molly.

More bats arrive, until there are **eight** flying overhead. Molly's sister and brothers disappear into their tents, scared out of their wits. Molly does not move. She watches as the bats circled, now **nineteen**, no, **twenty**!

"Hi, Molly," says her **mother**, walking up behind her **father** to the campfire.

"Wow, there sure are a lot of bats around these woods," says her dad. "Aren't you scared?"

Molly shook her head no, and watched the bats fly off into the starry night sky.

"Let's eat dinner!" she said. Her brothers and sister come out of their tents. The family eats by the fire. They love to camp together.

Molly is **twenty-two**. She just graduated from college, where she studied engineering. She has not found a job in an office, so she works at her local outdoor store. She saves her paycheck and gets to talk about her favorite hobby all day: camping.

Every Saturday, Molly works on the **second** floor, with all of the tents, backpacks, and camping supplies. This Saturday, in walks her **cousin**.

"Hi, Jim!" says Molly, a happy smile on her face.

"Molly! I forgot you work here," says Jim, the **thirty**-year-old **son** of Molly's **aunt** Jane.

"How are Aunt Jane and **Uncle** Joe?" asks Molly.

"They're good. This weekend they are visiting **Grandma** Gloria at her house," says Jim. "I'm here to buy some outdoor goods for a trip."

"Oh, sure! I can help you. What is on your list?" Molly asks.

Jim shows Molly a piece of paper with a list of **fifteen** items. A light backpack, a portable stove, **four** pairs of warm socks, hiking poles, Dr. Bronner's magic soap, a pocket knife, and **eighteen** dehydrated trail meals.

Wow, this sounds like quite a trip, thinks Molly.

"Gimme the lightest backpack you have," says Jim. "The lightest everything, actually. I have to keep my pack under **twenty-eight** pounds."

"What are you buying all of this for?" asks Molly, walking with Jim over to a wall filled with backpacks of all colors, large and small.

"I'm going to hike," says Jim. "Across Spain."

Jim tries on the different backpacks. He chooses Molly's favorite, a red backpack with **seven** pockets, four on the back and three inside. The pack is so light, it hardly weighs **two-and-a-half** pounds. He wears it on his shoulders as he follows Molly to the clothing section.

"It's called the Camino de Santiago," Jim tells Molly. Her cousin tells her about the hike. It is a pilgrimage to the Cathedral of Santiago de Compostela in Galicia. People say that Saint James is buried in the church.

Uncle Jim will be walking the hike from the common starting point of the French Way, Saint-Jean-Pied-de-Port. From there, it is about **five hundred** miles to Santiago. The pilgrimage has been popular since the Middle Ages. Criminals and other people walked the way in exchange for blessings. Nowadays, most travel by foot. Some people travel by bicycle. A few pilgrims even travel on a horse or donkey. The pilgrimage was religious, but now many do it for travel or sport.

"I need to travel," says Jim. "I need time to think and reflect. Walking 500 miles can be very spiritual."

Molly helps Jim find a waterproof jacket and a pair of pants that can unzip to be shorts. He seems very happy with his large bag of things. He has much more in his hands than the other shoppers. He is going on a real trip.

"That will be **three hundred forty-seven** dollars and **sixty-six** cents," says Molly.

"Thanks, Molly," says Jim.

Molly begins to think. She lives at home with her **parents**. Her mother works as a judge in the local courthouse and her father is a lawyer. They are both rarely home for dinner. They stay busy at the office until late. Her **siblings** live with their families in Seattle, three hours away. She is alone, with no real job. She has no one to stop her.

It will be the perfect vacation. And maybe she will decide what to do with the rest of her life.

Why not?

That day, Mollly decides that she will do the Camino de Santiago. Starting in September, three months from now. Alone.

CONCLUSION

You did it!

You finished a whole book in a brand new language. That in and of itself is quite the accomplishment, isn't it?

Congratulate yourself on time well spent and a job well done. Now that you've finished the book, you have familiarized yourself with over 500 new vocabulary words, comprehended the heart of 3 short stories, and listened to loads of dialogue unfold, all without going anywhere!

Charlemagne said "To have another language is to possess a second soul." After immersing yourself in this book, you are broadening your horizons and opening a whole new path for yourself.

Have you thought about how much you know now that you did not know before? You've learned everything from how to greet and how to express your emotions to basics like colors and place words. You can tell time and ask question. All without opening a schoolbook. Instead, you've cruised through fun, interesting stories and possibly listened to them as well.

Perhaps before you weren't able to distinguish meaning when you listened to German. If you used the audiobook, we bet you can now pick out meanings and words when you hear someone speaking. Regardless, we are sure you have taken an important step to being more fluent. You are well on your way!

Best of all, you have made the essential step of distinguishing in your mind the idea that most often hinders people studying a new language. By approaching German through our short stories and dialogs, instead of formal lessons with just grammar and vocabulary, you are no longer in the 'learning' mindset. Your approach is much more similar to an osmosis, focused on speaking and using the language, which is the end goal, after all!

So, what's next?

This is just the first of five books, all packed full of short stories and dialogs, covering essential, everyday German that will ensure you master the basics. You can find the rest of the books in the series, as well as a whole host of other resources, at LearnLikeNatives.com. Simply add the book to your library to take the next step in your language learning journey. If you are ever in need of new ideas or direction, refer to our 'Speak Like a Native' eBook, available to you for free at LearnLikeNatives.com, which clearly outlines practical steps you can take to continue learning any language you choose.

We also encourage you to get out into the real world and practice your German. You have a leg up on most beginners, after all—instead of pure textbook learning, you have been absorbing the sound and soul of the language. Do not underestimate the foundation you have built reviewing the chapters of this book. Remember, no one feels 100% confident when they speak with a native speaker in another language.

One of the coolest things about being human is connecting with others. Communicating with someone in their own language is a wonderful gift. Knowing the language turns you into a local and opens up your world. You will see the reward of learning languages for many years to come, so keep that practice up!. Don't let your fears stop you from taking the chance to use your German. Just give it a try, and remember that you will make mistakes. However, these mistakes will teach you so much, so view every single one as a small victory! Learning is growth.

Don't let the quest for learning end here! There is so much you can do to continue the learning process in an organic way, like you did with this book. Add another book from Learn Like a Native to your library. Listen to German talk radio. Watch some of the great German Musical. Put on the latest CD from Sarah Connor. Take cooking lessons in German. Whatever you do, don't stop because every little step you take counts towards learning a new language, culture, and way of communicating.

www.LearnLikeNatives.com

Learn Like a Native is a revolutionary **language education brand** that is taking the linguistic world by storm. Forget boring grammar books that never get you anywhere, Learn Like a Native teaches you languages in a fast and fun way that actually works!

As an international, multichannel, language learning platform, we provide **books, audio guides and eBooks** so that you can acquire the knowledge you need, swiftly and easily.

Our **subject-based learning**, structured around real-world scenarios, builds your conversational muscle and ensures you learn the content most relevant to your requirements. Discover our tools at ***LearnLikeNatives.com***.

When it comes to learning languages, we've got you covered!